THE **FORTUNATE ERA**

THE **FORTUNATE ERA**

POEMS BY
Arthur Smith

carnegie mellon university press
PITTSBURGH 2013

ACKNOWLEDGMENTS

Grateful acknowledgment is made to the editors of the following publications for poems that originally appeared in them:

Atlanta Review ("Main Street, Milky Way" and "War News"); *American Literary Review* ("Before the Absolute" and "Tracking Down the Music of the Spheres"); *Bat City Review* ("Church" under the title "Endanger"); *Crazyhorse* ("Annuals," "In Sickness and in Health," and "Charm" under the title "Because There Is"); *Cutthroat: A Journal of the Arts* ("Cuttings," "Reconsidering Joyce," "Riverrun," "The Usual Is What You Get," "Walter's Eternity," and "What Gods"); *descant* ("High Summer" ["It's hard to believe in only"] and "Rock Garden"); *The Georgia Review* ("Constant Sorrow," "Paradise," "Valentine," and "Zeno's Sparrow"); *Great River Review* ("Lives of the Poet" and "Of All Things"); *Hunger Mountain* ("What Song Hath the Creatures of the Field?"); *New Millennium Writings* ("In Memory of the Georgia Sun"); *Northwest Review* ("Sans Soleil," "Schrödinger's Dog," and "What I Staked What Was Left of My Life On"); *The Pinch* ("San Fran,"); *Poems and Plays* ("Of All People" under the title "A Place in Time for This, Too," and "The Future Is Already Among Us, The Old Man Said"); *Sonora Review* ("Ars Poetica"); *Southern Poetry Review* ("Golden Gate" and "Goodbye to the Isle of Palms"); *TriQuarterly Review* ("The Cardinals of Zen," "Matinee," and "We Have Made These Things").

Thanks are due to the English Department of the University of Tennessee for a research leave during which a number of these poems were written or begun, and for a grant from the University of Tennessee Office of Research.

Special thanks to David Kitchel, Julia Levine, Amy Billone, Jesse Graves, Marilyn Kallet, Curt Rode, Michael Starry, Austin Duck, Conrad Discont, Patricia Waters, Bradford Tice, John and Marta Gray.

I especially want to thank my wife Mary McGarvey for her support and encouragement.

Book design by Joanne Ong

Library of Congress Control Number 2012938564
ISBN 978-0-88748-567-1

10   9   8   7   6   5   4   3   2   1

for Stanley Plumly
and
in memory of William Matthews

Lissener hispert, 'Whats the matter?'

I hispert back, 'O what we ben! And what we come to!'
Boath of us wer sniffling and snuffling then. Me looking at them jynt
machines and him lissening ther sylents. . . . How cud any 1 not want
to get that shyning Power back from time back way back? How cud any
1 not want to be like them what had boats in the air and picters on the
wind? How cud any 1 not want to see them shyning weals terning?

— RUSSELL HOBAN, *Riddley Walker*

CONTENTS

PART 1: GOLDEN GATE

PARADISE

I used to live there, I was born there, every morning
The downtown streets were cobbled with gold, honey
Flowed—all that stuff. I'm not kidding. Summers
Lasted a lifetime, broken by Christmas
And New Year's.
Mornings, like waking to someone's scent
You hadn't yet met and married for life,
Though I didn't know that then—the night-cooled
Muskmelons rolling belly-up to the stars,
And by late afternoon the dusk-colored
Dust of apricots on everything.
From that earth, my body
Assembled itself, and when the veil dropped,
I tried to say what I saw. The light winds
Around me died, the sheers of summer wavered
As though all of it were mirage. Cantaloupes,
Grapes, clusters of ruby flames, like champagne,
Though I didn't know that then—
Nectarines like morphine, nor that.
Oranges, almonds, rainbows,
Tangs—rolling in all year long, that bounty.
You tell people that, over and over,
And it's really crazy, they won't believe you.
All that sugar coaxed out of clay and you
Can't even give it away—and each dawn more
Was just piled on. I took in as much
As I could, like larder, and walked away.

CHURCH

About to be fewer by one are those few
Sanctuaries in North America
Where you can sit on the crumbling trunk of a bull-pine
Broken by lightning or wind or whim

And at twilight hear Holsteins shoo
The slower calves before them
On a cow path on the far side of the river,
And the neighbor's bantams picketing something,
        always picketing something.

I love a woman who has bad dreams, a vision
Of the world with no great cats—
And so frost-crack or sun-burn, whatever weather,
Once a week, every week, starting

In darkness she shovels it up
And hoses it down,
The den housings blanched to a cloud-color
Steaming in the morning sun.

The work makes her invisible—
Lions and tigers
Stretching and yawning,
Huffing

Flare-nostriled in the cooling air,
The lions bellowing back and forth, like bullfrogs across
        a pond,
Their dread-manes mossy and swaying
The way trees sway, laden with cicadas—

The sticky bricks of horse meat tossed in
In late afternoon,
Two huge Siberians, powerless ghosts,
Trailing her without a sound.

MATINEE

He can't believe
This is love,
Or the same tire-rutted road home
He walked out on

Only a couple of hours ago,
Or that he doesn't mind walking
The same tire-rutted road
Home by himself. Now he can see

There is this other light—
In it, even the dust
Scuffed up
Looks just like

Rust on his shoes, or suede.
On one side of him, a bounty of late calves
Schooling in a field.
On the other, a carnival of sheared cane stalks

Sizzling.
                    Everything he looks at
Looks back—
The green fires snapping low to the ground
And the cloddish ash

The earth turns sweet on—the calves mewling,
The blunt stalks
Steaming, the steady heat
And smoke so like

His own mind smoldering
With her—
              What a trip,
He is thinking, walking along,
Reeled in.

LIVES OF THE POET

For some of us there were many years of living past
Anyone we would have died for.

Many moved, moved often, often at night, never moved.
Because we had to, because we couldn't, because we insisted on
        helping ourselves, packing a little less each time.

Living on the run, lifting plums, casabas, as many eggs
        as she could make off with
Without them cracking in her swaddled shirt.

Another, all his adult life lived in a cave
Where he wore out seven suits of armor in his battles with the Devil—

At the end of the day, the gruesome work at his feet,
        slain demons
No one could see.

                Not unlike that off-white ruffled blouse
        (sun-warmed and wind-stiffened)

One of us unpinned
From a pretty neighbor's clothesline

And wore from time to time in his own small room
And could never mention to any one.

SANS SOLEIL

Once in the future, in an underground cramped city
Below the frozen one that used to be Toronto, I found
Myself walking through nurseries drizzling
With ferns and banks of pink azaleas.
There were mortuaries and mute
White camellias for a hearse. There were hearses.
There were bodegas, and strawberries
Overnighted from New Zealand.
I bought a dozen vanilla bean pods
Stoppered in a slender glass bottle,
My nose hooked in Madagascar.
There was more than one pet store overrun with parrots,
Like beach apartments for the festive insane. I watched
A young black woman beat her teenaged son
With the shoe she had just then stooped
To step out of. Every one slowed and circled.
Other voices walked by in Chinese, in what sounded
Like Portuguese, something Swedish. The boy
Was taller and outweighed her. He covered his ears
And the back of his head and took every blow
She had in her. The mother's rage at all of us watching,
The boy's acquiescence to whatever you want
To call this, the Arctic eating any hope
Of life above the surface. What can you do? This is the way
The world is going to work. Down here, everything occurs
In the present, now, which happens over and over
Because that's all we have.
She is berating him in French. You can tell
By the sound it has a wooden sole.

BEFORE THE ABSOLUTE

Before there was the speed of light
There wasn't. It's that simple,
The stargazers say.

Before there was your original face,
Even then there was no before.
Any one's face tells you that.

The same way the power-grid blows—whoosh,
It's gone—
The light sucked back up even faster

By the darkness it burst from. First night
Moving in, new house on hands and knees
On the stairwell, I'm alone, exhausted, a bit giddy,

And it's late when it goes, and just as suddenly
I had something like a vision.
I don't know what I was thinking,

But I was jerked up like a fish and hoisted
So far up in the air
I could see how all the houses down there lived long
        before me,

And even before the houses, how the land belonged
To the sun-powered pines, hill after
        hill of them,
And before the pines, before the hills,

Before every single thing else,
Only water and the wind roughhousing over it,
Only water and only the wind making it look alive.

WAR NEWS

Just try avoiding it and see what happens.
There are televisions on every wrist, every wall,
You hear them everywhere you go,
The grim news like white background,

Like breathing or counting, or
Not having to keep count. Like looking
At your sister's house by satellite,
Her gazebo a brown blur on the yellowed lawn,

So when the photograph was taken
She was living. There is a red car
Parked in front of the house.
Probably someone from the government

Giving everything an official name,
Like *mycobacterium avium complex.*
By the time you figure out what is
Being said, your sister is dead.

HIGH SUMMER

It's hard to believe in only
The minions of existence,

Each thing crawling
Or burrowing—all that winged

Whispering below understanding.
Now that my father has

Died, I have said only
A few words

Over the body of his grave.
I'm like the dog dozing,

Her paws
Nodding like bobbers

In the unease
Of a dream's current.

Out the back door
The lawn is still bermuda,

And whatever
The broad oaks utter

When the gusts test them
Is not a lullaby

Not a name.

WHAT SONG HATH THE CREATURES OF THE FIELD?

Rabbits are aware when they are
About to have their throats slit.
They know when you walk back
To the cage with that in mind.

What a rotten feeling if your heart's
Not in it. They squeal with a voice
That doesn't belong to Easter,
But to a small, terrified mammal.

I loved it when my mother baked—
That was before she worked—
Something sugary and moist like
Mainline cake from someone else's hand.

While she baked she sang—
What a friend we have, and lonesome
Valleys, and being by yourself in a place
You would never have recognized

By yourself.

TRACKING DOWN THE MUSIC
OF THE SPHERES

You can hear it in real minutes, in faint
Gear-clicks, in the crisp
Scooping sound
A star-nose mole makes shredding
A nightcrawler.
In things that can't be heard, too, the static
The mind makes of death so close
At hand. You can feel it as the long day
Wavers into night, parading over
A line of ginkgoes, those moon-fringed leaves
Chirping back and forth like seagoing birds.
Their secret? Patience, perseverance,
How to live another hundred thousand
Summers in a heartbeat.
When you can see that far ahead,
You look back and find all the present
Everywhere in ruins, the world you knew
Having lasted only a little longer
Than you did—the new world like dust
On top of the old.
This coal-driven city, the lights in its head
Knocked down for hours now—beacons, business towers,
Dark facades—
You can feel it in the neighborhood park,
The wind almost hushed, breezes teasing
A blindfolded swing, in the black-windowed
Downtown, too—time flying through it.

ROCK GARDEN

The Zen Buddhists are making fun
Of the sitting Buddhists again.

!

        They are saying
You can't polish
A brick into being a mirror,
No matter how long
You rub it with your butt.

!

They point at their brothers and laugh,
And then laugh again at their pointing.

!

The sitters, also in Japanese,
Smile
And go on rubbing.

!

All this time, and all our knowing
Is no closer to everything
We can't account for in ourselves.

!

What terrible hunger,
To crave meaning
From rocks.

THE TRUTH

People would rather
Complain. About
Anything—the soaring cost
Of caviar, the "heinie" virus,
Any virus, about vaccines
For viruses, any vaccines,
About drywall from China.
Milk from China.
Anything from China.
About pine nuts from China
Sold by "Woodpine Farms"
Of Oakland, California.
About traffic cameras
That nab you running reds
And street cams
Filtering every thought.
About Muslims, meth heads, the killing
Of seal pups. Even Jesus.
There wasn't anything
Wrong with Jesus.
He lived. He looked
Into our hearts and found
Them crooked. He wandered
The warrens our hard-wired minds make
And found a few new ways
To praise it all.
The truth is
When he died he broke
His mother's crooked
Little heart.

THE FUTURE IS ALREADY AMONG US

By the time it's tracked down,
The last clouded leopard
Will have died of peritonitis
In a sanctuary in east Tennessee.

That's my guess. It could happen.
In the ancient world I might have been
Taken for a seer. I could have asked
For honey and roe, and a Lamborghini,

And a blonde on each arm, twins,
Like the old man had.
I'd been reading about chimeras
When I thought of the rare cloudeds,

Those smooth movers,
Like sleek boas over the thick limbs.
What an immense silence they make.
You don't notice it at first.

THE CARDINALS OF ZEN

So. Once a year the earth
Rubs around the sun
A sound so low
Only the physical world can hear it.
The red-tailed hawks hear it,
Roosting as they are this year
In the neighbor's streetside pine.
Thus, the seasons orbit the backyard pool and deck
And put out the call for chlorine.
By this we think we outwit death.
But no one's fooled.
The cardinal, the damn cardinal, we sigh,
Is back at it, attacking every cardinal
That looks just like it—all spring and summer—
Reared up in the sunroom windows.
It must be dealt with.
We are old friends just talking
On the shaded deck of an early
Morning spring.
We've been around. We keep opening our eyes.
One of the hawks could plunge & pull up, hovering,
And the cardinal in the roses right now—
In a flash—in the hawk's
Hooks in the dirt,
That ruby air misting our faces,
Our fluttering hearts, amen.

ZENO'S SPARROW

He walks into a thin morning
Of mist over the low
Appalachians—and already
A wheat-feathered sparrow
In the wheelwell of his car,
After bug-nuggets, seeds,
Whatnots
In tread and mud, the little
They live on, and where
In the deadend of winter
They find it. Someone's friend
Is being slid
Into the side of a hill somewhere near here
Forever this afternoon.
Someone always is, but this one's
One of his,
And the difference
Is
His steps in the gravel
Seem so slowed right now,
The moment so riddled, his mind
Blinking at so much light,
That most of what he'll remember
Is a long morning spent
Walking toward
A blue car
A sparrow's feeding on.

OF ALL THINGS

In Colombia one of the rarely seen tribes
Surprised the town's public square.
The men were bony, only a few
Children, the women
Stared at the earth in front of them.
No one was more
Haunted than their leader.

Weeks of marching through the rain forest,
Chased by rebels, *dopistas,* landmongers.
Chased away from the forest floor
They had picked over forever for berries and roots,
For the curare leaves they used in hunting.

Small monkeys blow-darted
From the trees were sometimes still living
When their heads were roasted.

Now how will we live, he asked—
This, in the language
Of a people who lack a word for the future.

Of all things, love lacks a word
For the future, and so dies in a clearing.

You come to, naked, gray rocks on fire all around.
There is nowhere else to go.

No one will know
What you are talking about,
No one will know the song.

Never again that delicacy,
The two of you.

THE STORIED HILL YOU WALK ME UP

I keep wondering, walking,
Whether it's only to share
This blusteringly sere peak of a hill
And the bleak building crowning it
I told you I already knew—the one wind-buffed
And spotlighted with marble faces leering
From the brick arches as only a few Romans
Might have been cruel enough
To press into art.
When I look to ask you
What it is you want, your face
Is so rinsed
With the marble's envy
It's like that moment
Just before we met,
When I turned down the dust of a hallway
I would have sworn empty
And you were standing there stopped in front of me—
Just before *that*—when all I was
Was rooted
To an even barer place
Scoured by a night winter wind
Bearing I didn't know what
From somewhere else.

WALTER'S ETERNITY

It's always early summer
Inside me—or late spring, birthdays,

The slightest breath of dew still
Mist on the rose leaves, bouquet

Of apricots and dates more
Redolent in the morning

Open to the world.
Me too. The towering

Palm trees pigeonholed with pigeons
Crapping on anyone trying

To get to their ramshackle nests.
The old man two houses down

With my father's name, I would see him
As I climbed the tall palms—

Always walking the streets, with purpose,
The blocks back and forth, the grid

A city's laid out on, his pants cinched up
Mid-chest though I never made

Fun of him, his hunched walk, his back
Broken in an earthquake, a fact

I learned in school he lived
Through in 1906 when he was six.

Hard to imagine. I know a woman
Who fled Bosnia when the hostilities

Intensified. She was a child.
Age means nothing. Age means

You're counting. Is there an end
To sadness? However long

We wander the streets, here away
From the bay area, away from a homeland,

Looking for our mothers,
Sisters, fathers, lovers, the ruins

Of our lives burning in the fires, in the rubble,
In the work of living, in my mind.

PART 2: DELICACIES

VALENTINE

Back then, for all I cared,
God could have been a spider
Glossy as a buttercup
Sunning in the garden
Of the first woman
Time gave me to
And then took back.

What I mean is, once, like ice,
Something pierced my heart
With a light
So fierce
It heightened
Every thin-stemmed flower after.

That's how I think of God now,
Each time—
Going back to her—
That immense and holy cold, an arrow
Sinking in.

MAIN STREET, MILKY WAY

In the long convalescence following
My wife's death
I lived only a three-block walk
From the Menil Museum in Houston.
The same walk took me
To the Rothko Chapel where God was
Made invisible to me—even the dumb
Rocks hid Him.
Just in front of the Chapel
Was Barnett Newman's massive obelisk
Upside down,
Like an angel's plumb bob
Snapped off
And stuck in that cooling fountain spray
That was always worth
Walking to,
A little pleasure
Left over from creation.
I wasn't the only one who thought so—
Every day, couples, or one by one,
Many of them slowing around the fountain.
At dusk, common swifts
Swept those mists free of damselflies and gnats—
All of them holy, not one of them
Mattering,
No one knowing.

WHAT I STAKED WHAT WAS LEFT OF MY LIFE ON

I was as low as I
        had ever been, but not
                as low as the downstairs

Black Vietnam vet
        on dialysis, legally blind,
                one-legged, for two days

Picked over by beetles
        greener than emeralds.
                I was between lives, too,

But even with the sorrows
        I harbored—
                widowed, ghost-married—

Even grief
        like that again, I knew
                I would break down any door

To get more of it.
        Every night I learned a little solace
                from the street lamp's

Glow and coldness.
        Some evenings fogged in,
                other nights I could see

All the way out
        to the cold rubble tumbling
                over and over, never catching up

With the light it was once part of.
        Outside the window
                every night—cloud-burst

Or full moon—you could count on it—
        tree roaches glistening like caramel
                on the mulberry's limbs,

Up and down they would go
        on the slick trunk. Up and down
           the soft limbs.

Houston, 1981

CONSTANT SORROW

After a few years, the dreams
Died too, ones that had me
Cooped-up inside someone else's
Car, a train, an almost always
Empty bus. Each time the screen door
Opening and her watching
From a bungalow shadowed by elms,
My face flattened against the cold window
For a long time looking back. Thirty
Years. Funerals, friendships, everyone
Weathered, romance and debris. But twice
This week now she has walked into
The graveled yard and stood there, young,
While I found myself
On the far side of the heavy traffic,
No longer in it. Both times it was
As though we were neighbors. I nodded.
It was hot in the yard. I was weeding
Or doodling, a man kneeling
In the garden of his own mind.
Each time I looked, she flickered
Between the trucks and vans. Trying
To say something, I thought,
Because near the end she couldn't
And I could only watch her blinking
As she tried. I had forgotten
That. *I can't hear you,* I nodded
Back. *I still can't.*

IN SICKNESS AND IN HEALTH

No wonder the poems flew out of me faster
Than they could be accounted for—it was
Starting all over like heaven or home
Wherever she turned my head, living with her.

No wonder now, too, in a world without her,
They're springing up out of what's left—
Each one a bright wall falling
Before I can prop it with another.

"SAN FRAN,"

The young man said
On New Year's Eve
In Knoxville—

In his words,
A story of dependence,
Exhaustion, drugs,

Some loved young thing
A long time dying.
And then remorse, since sooner

Or later
The dead come back.
I listened in someone

Else's house
To someone from a city
That wasn't the one I knew

Over forty years ago.
Veronica and I were just married.
No one we knew who lived there, who lived

With feeling for that place,
No one called it "San Fran"—
But things change,

Everything becomes something else.
Those days are alive inside me
Differently now, the insistent Pacific

Sea breezes freshening
At the salt lick of something constant,
She and I

On one of those slate-colored beaches the fog
Washed up there every morning,
Heartless and alive.

PART 3: **OF ALL THINGS**

WHAT GODS

The new world has been
Tough on everyone—the young
Adrift, numb
On chatter, the old
Living out a golden age,
The rest of us aligned with liars
Who lie to us, who tell us
The gods are now telling them
To tell us to bow down.
But all the while, underneath,
Something simple is being articulated,
Simple and furious, the way
Roots articulate, hungry
For the fat of the earth in front of them.
It's as simple as the junipers pooling
Toward evening, the long slide
From green to gray. All these years
I have watched this happen, and nothing
Has died in my heart.
Over two thousand miles away
My mother growing elderly in the deserts
Of California, tending a little fire,
Watching over
What's left of her husband
And daughter, something in the old woman
Deeper now, adamantine, not even needing the fire.
What now? it chuffs, puffing heat
Into her cupped hands. *Where to?*

GOODBYE TO THE ISLE OF PALMS

I had come too far to find
Solace in great error,
In the intertidal thoughts
Of that island beach.

One night I waded out
To where I was in
Over my head.
It was simpler than
I imagined.

For a while
There were constellations
The human night went on dragging overhead,
underfoot.

After that,
Names
Nothing answered to.

BREAKFAST FOR ONE

Emily Dickinson was
A loneliness in American thought
That reached out into itself.

Like Blake, she knew angels
Drowsed inside and out
And could be set smoldering
By great loss.

She knew they would strain
To unfurl the massive
Pair of stained glass wings inside her rib cage.

She knew the armature was classic
And made of pink marble.

She knew once it started moving
It would crush
Every bone in her body.

OF ALL PEOPLE

Learning to live in the city, you don't
Have to walk out under the heavens
The last thing each night to feel diminished
By the far-off stars.

                          Even if it's raining,
Those lights are up there,
The same way our childhoods are somewhere.

The same way my sister languishes
Somewhere in the western desert,
Devoured
                 by microscopic blue-green plants
Whose fronds made tatters of her lungs
And married her forever to the sands.

Somewhere Barry Manilow is blowing her a kiss
From a white limousine flying by us
On a steep grade in the mountains
Between the deserts
Of Reno and South Lake Tahoe.

Of all people.

I had never seen her happier—
Beside herself,
         blowing kisses back.

GAME THEORY

All I'm saying
Is soon
There will be no one to talk with
About those days

When parents
Told their children
That children who played games
Went to hell.

They said games
Were for children. The children—
Like me and Sister,
Who was the grandmother

You'll never know—we said,
But we *are* children!
They didn't care. No radio, books,
No names, no games, no building blocks.

The summer I was six,
The summer we lived just outside
Paradise in the oleander
Homeless jungles on either side

Of the old highway, Mother
Made us pick cotton that grew
Like weeds in the abandoned lots
You'd find in any town

With ghosts. Four pennies
For each long burlap sack
Stuffed with it. Life was not
Bad. You made do—

Sister and I lying
When asked
If we'd been playing or singing
Under our breath.

GOLDEN GATE

All the known jumpers off the Golden Gate
Chose to face the known Bay
And not the towering cold Pacific.
There are witnesses. You can understand

Wanting to, trembling out there
On braided cables, wind-whipped
Hundreds of feet in the air. From that height,
Water has the density of rock. It's surprising

A handful have lived. Any one of them
Would tell you jumping is an act
You have time to reconsider.
In a heartbeat, they knew.

WE HAVE MADE THESE THINGS

If you back off far enough,
High above the earth, you can see almost
Everything—at least almost half
Of almost everything.

You can see a middle-school boy
Gut-shot
By a serial sniper in an upscale
Suburb outside Washington DC,
And think of it as one more item
In the news of a grisly world.

                                        Or from a camera
Near the nose cone,
Re-wind and witness yourself
Lifting off, like the shuttle—
The earth jacked back, the known earth
Receding as though blown away.

It's easier now to see
How the earth churns in orbit,
And how, once in a while,
It wobbles.

The kid lived, lucky or not.
The crew didn't.

The sniper turned out to be
A tag team, two blacks demanding
A ransom to stop. They popped women
And children and men. They smacked
Yellows and whites and reds and blacks. They crippled
The affluent as eagerly as they maimed the poor.

Luck had
Nothing to do with those two.
They were in it, they confessed, for the money.

The truth is, they liked their work
And would have labored without pay—

You can see at least
Half of that from here.

THE USUAL IS WHAT YOU GET

A full house tonight, no seconds
On the hash browns before they go cold.
Soup spoons and forks, water glasses,
The meal chatter we can't not make
When gathered eating, and behind that,
A woman's voice, a foreign war's mumble
From a big-box television bolted to the wall.
Dawn here, she says, *the usual: a dozen males,*
Hands something *wires,*
And then something something else,
And then I can't hear her anymore
Because of the noise.
It's disturbing how much of the awful is getting through,
How little of the disturbing. Day by day,
How much more little.

ARS POETICA

A musket ball burrows through a body
Pulverizing every bone it's introduced to—
Later, bone-powder caking on a saw blade,
Arms in a heap, as though lolling,
A leg dropped into a large metal bucket.

"A horrible sound," he recalled years later.
"I had to listen to it as I helped them
Write their loved ones." Walt Whitman,

A sun umbrella going tent
To tent in the outdoor surgical wards—
Sitting with the mutilated, the soon
To be discharged, wild flowers all around
Cheering spring on.

SCHRÖDINGER'S DOG

It's troubling, looking back, how
Easily worded into war
We were, and later everyone lamenting
How we should have known better
Than to trust a man
Who would have had a beer
With the likes of us. For some
Of us—me, I mean—innocence
Ended in the 1950s
In my own back yard—Sputnik
Half a world ago. By there,
I mean earth Eden, the slender
Green valley of California
You can stand in the middle of—
Say Fresno or Madera—
And see the mountains on both
Sides walling all of it in.
At night, lying in the damp
Crabgrass, up in the sky a dog
Among the stars, we wondered
How they were going to get
Her down. How quaint that wondering
Seems, the same way war conventions
Seem. Who would have thought
Iraq would make me homesick
For the desert I was born
Into, all those tall date palms
Like street lamps for the daytime
Hours, a summer dusk like dust
Sifting down, a collar
Of pigeon shit and feathers around
Each trunk? During the months

The field workers were in the country
There was so much food no one
Went hungry. Sweet yellow ears
Of corn, and pomegranates, kumquats,
All four hundred varieties
Of tomatoes, squash, string beans,
Honeydews—all of it, and
All the rest, half the produce
Of an entire nation.
Who would have imagined Hmong-
Grown strawberries like plum
Ambrosia? Or watermelons
Shaped like boxes you could stack
And later crack open
On the lawn and dig into
The spongy orange flesh inside?

RECONSIDERING JOYCE

A man is thinking, *Jesus,*
It wouldn't have taken much
To flush.
He's thinking
The milky sea-green marble walls
Agree with him,
But it's only echo.
He's alone, peeing,
Thinking out loud
In a mall's men's room.
He's wishing he weren't so quick to criticize.
Wishing he had the patience of history, of having
Seen it all already,
Of being
All right with the welling up
Of the next world war, as James Joyce was
Just before he died
Of broken teeth, and blindness,
And a bleeding ulcer, alone
In Zurich, fleeing Hitler.

What a rotten life.

Proud to have written a book
No one could read.

ANNUALS

I couldn't even tell you
Why I was so afraid
The night we were being married facing
The wind out over the ocean
On a pier near Charleston.
Although I did manage to tell you
That I was.
Every dread I had ever run across
Was nourishing inside me, in the desert
I carry everywhere inside me.
When I looked past you to the sea,
There were brilliants beyond counting
Being chalked on its surface by the moon—
Sun after sun, and stars, and moons,
And equally as many falling stars—
Pooling over and over again
Back down.
Overwhelming plenitude
And underlying meaninglessness,
It's taken me this long to understand
It was the world
You were offering me.
At that moment I felt nothing
But terror inside,
And then within that terror,
Another life.

WHO LIGHTS YOUR WINDOWS?

Sweetness so late at night,
And so sweet to let it go in sleep,
Her leg over his, the dogs between them,
On top of them, all of them off duty.

From even one house away
The magnitude of the moment is invisible—

The neighborhood is down,
The lights out,
Nothing but candlepower
Making the windows shimmer.

HIGH SUMMER

When the dog is so knocked out
Her legs tremble,
I lower her name across the room.
I would like
To be able to say
Whatever is calming.
The broad oaks don't need to do this,
Banked on the high side of the hill
Behind the house.
Scout, I say. Scout,
In that dry field,
Among those weeds.

IN MEMORY OF THE GEORGIA SUN

Nothing looks the same—
A three-hour drive in which the car
Is light-pierced and sun-crushed.
The roadside seed-topped weed stalks
We sweep past
Like cilia embracing nothing.
These might be the houses Whitman meant—
Clustered near the road, isolated farther back—
To kick the doors from the jambs
And the jambs themselves from the walls—
The old wood siding sun-wowed, like tinder, the shacks
No one has lived in for years.
Today a friend of mine is being buried
By her mother,
Wavering with the rest of us
On a narrow terraced slope of Myrtle Hill,
One of Rome's seven.
Everyone knows
Spring is not going to be held back
One whit because of this.
There is a yellow
Resin already falling,
Sifting over everything—dark suits,
The women's hats, the gray tent.
Even if that butter of spring
Gets sour on you,
Even if you wash your face,
Some is left behind.

CUTTINGS

Sometimes nothing helps.
That's why we are so many.
We can't all root and shine
With what we find.

Same with the runners from the spider plant,
The *madre malo,*
A few live just because.

This morning the little they have found
Is the kitchen linoleum floor
They have fallen to,
Sparely leafed, between worlds.

RIVERRUN

To someone from a rough river city
Like Pittsburgh or Paris,
The Tennessee may look demure, here where it begins
With the smaller French Broad jostling the Holston.

What sometimes happens here happens
Somewhere else all the time.
Into her, some are being driven, some pulled.

In the morning a man who slept under the south-side
          bridge supports woke
And climbed out on the bridge
And jumped. He was 27: it was
Christmas morning: it was
All over the news.

One of the human achievements—a day, a person,
An act—making something more important than it is.

Next day
Me and a friend sitting ruffled up in our coats on a riverside
          balcony,
The wrought-iron kind the wind whets its tongue on—
And then just as quickly the clouds crack open
And we're sheathed in a warmth, like light,
Like yolks in a shell.

CHARM

Because there is
   more to the self
Than the self can
   account for, I stop
Between the North Tyger
   and the South where it
Sluices under
   the interstate, its riverbanks
Foaming with poppies
   red and white like
The sides of parade floats.
   A few miles one way
Or the other, the Eastern
   Continental Divide—
Further proof
   I have never known
Which way was up—
   or for that matter,
Whom to please,
   what to avoid.
In some minds
   I have pretty much
Fucked up my life.
   All I am doing is
Taking a breather
   with whatever's next.

DEDICATIONS

Poems in this collection are dedicated
to the following individuals:

"Paradise"	Julia Levine
"Church"	Bubba, an African lion
"Sans Soleil"	Chris Marker, *"La Jetée"*
"War News"	Karen Luz
"The Future Is Already Among Us, The Old Man Said"	Mary Lynn Haven
"The Cardinals of Zen"	Al Braselton
"Walter's Eternity"	Walter Smith and Ena Djordjevič
"What Gods"	Iris Smith
"Of All People"	Manny Luz
"Game Theory"	Ryan Luz
"Who Lights Your Windows?"	Mary McGarvey
"In Memory of the Georgia Sun"	Jeanne Braselton
"Riverrun"	Jack Gilbert
"High Summer"	Scout McGarvey
"Charm"	Sheldon Glashow, *"the fortunate era . . . in which there is matter"*